HELLO CELLO POSITIONS!

2nd Position Book

By Jisoo Ok

for Young Cellists

First edition June 2020

ISBN 978-1-7350859-0-6

www.hellocellobooks.com

Other Publications by Jisoo Ok:

Hello Cello Positions! Second Position
Hello Cello Positions! Third Position
Hello Cello Positions! Fourth Position

Available at amazon.com

Accompaniment tracks available at hellocellobooks.com

Author's Note

While experienced cellists have developed a firm understanding of the importance of navigating the fingerboard through years of training, beginners, especially young students, often struggle with the process of learning and understanding fingerboard positions.

Despite years of searching for the right guide to teach the neck positions, I was unable to find a suitable book designed for young cellists that explained the positions in a comprehensive, yet fun and easy-to-understand, manner.

It is through my passion to help my cello students learn the positions in a simple and fun way that this book was born.

I would like to thank my amazing students, Emma, Alyssa, Juliet, Darcy and Aarika, for inspiring me to write this book! Thanks to Agnes Kwasniewska for introducing me to these wonderful students at the Virtuoso Suzuki Academy.

I am eternally grateful to all my former cello teachers - Kim Young-Suk, James Tennant, Natalia Pavlutskaya, Fred Sherry and Bonnie Hampton. I am thankful to Pamela Devenport for teaching Suzuki philosophies and methods of cello teaching with a unique and masterful approach.

Special thanks to my cousin, Isabel Kwon, a Juilliard trained cellist, for her advice and insights and to my brother-in-law John Ahn for helping me with editing and proofreading. Finally, to my family, my husband Hector, my son Santiago, my sister Krystal, and my parents for their love and support.

I had so much fun composing and arranging the pieces in this book!
I hope you have as much fun learning and playing them!

Enjoy!
Jisoo Ok

Content

Hello Extended Second Position on G string

Hello Extended Second Position on C string

Hello Lower Second Position on A string

Hello Lower Second Position on D string

Hello Lower Second Position on G string

Hello Lower Second Position on C string

2nd Position Review Party!

Cello Map

Closed Hand Position
Half steps between each fingers

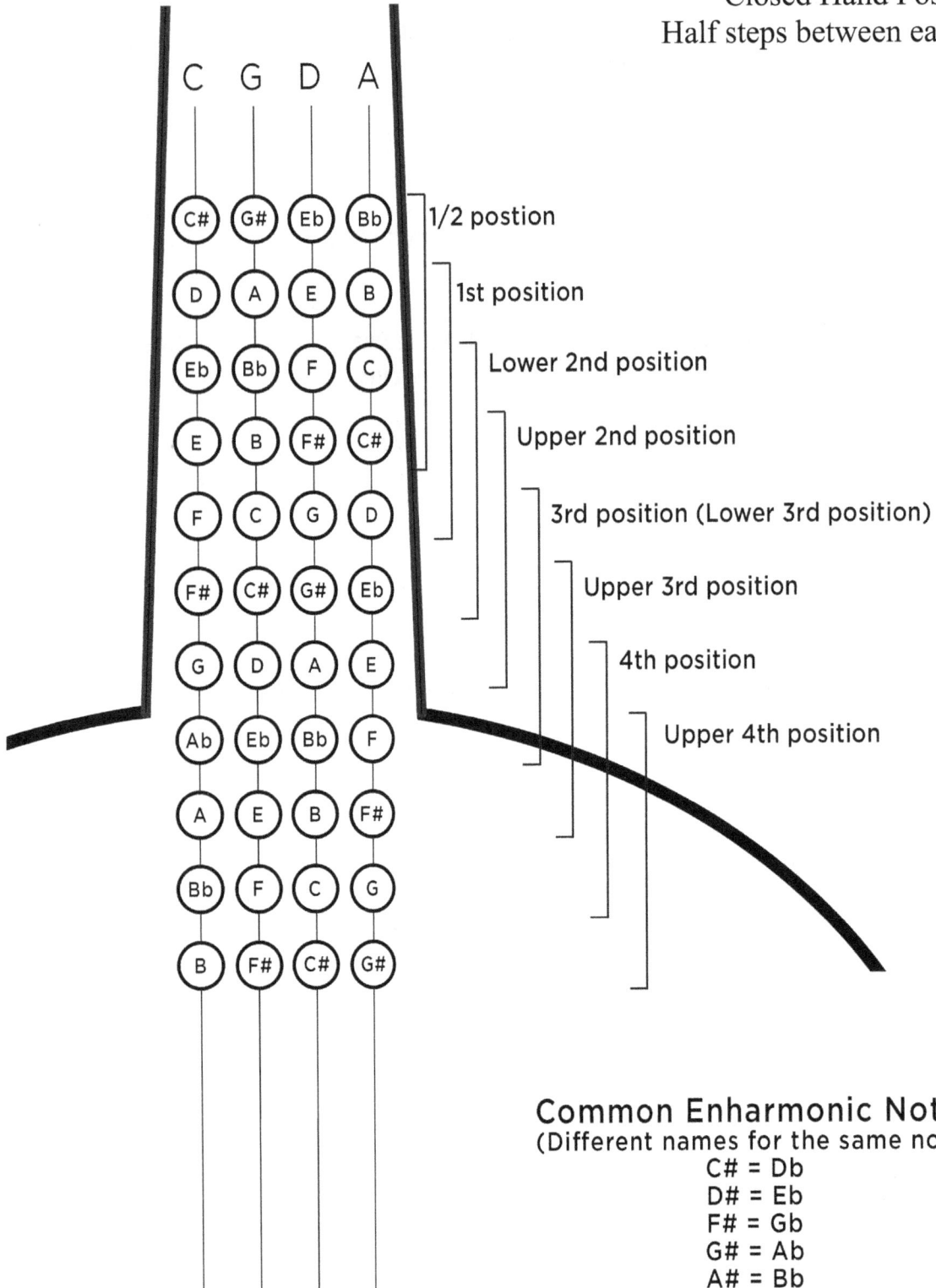

C G D A

Notes	Position
C# G# Eb Bb	1/2 postion
D A E B	1st position
Eb Bb F C	Lower 2nd position
E B F# C#	Upper 2nd position
F C G D	3rd position (Lower 3rd position)
F# C# G# Eb	Upper 3rd position
G D A E	4th position
Ab Eb Bb F	Upper 4th position
A E B F#	
Bb F C G	
B F# C# G#	

Common Enharmonic Notes
(Different names for the same note)
C# = Db
D# = Eb
F# = Gb
G# = Ab
A# = Bb

Second Positions

Upper 2nd Position

Extended 2nd Position

Lower 2nd Position

Hello Upper 2nd Position on A string!

Upper 2nd Position

D   D   D   C#   D   D#   E

Greetings!

What's Your Name?

Can you name the notes?

Let's Have Fun!

Sleepy Sloth

Always check the
key signature

Silly Goose

6

Lazy Cat

Remember
your sharps

The Mischievous Puppy

Shooting Star

Hello Upper 2nd Position on D string!

Upper 2nd Position

0 4 2   1 2 3 4

G   G   G   F#   G   G#   A

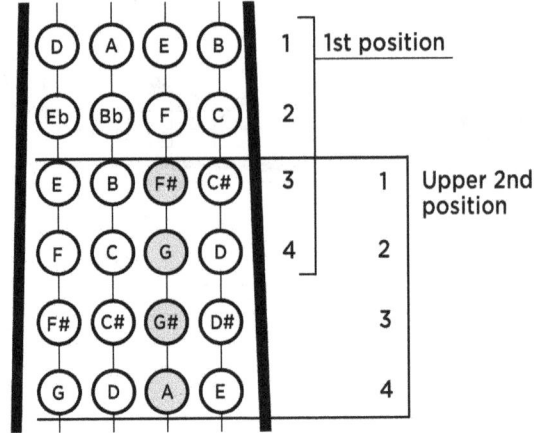

Greetings!

0   2   1   2   4   0   2   1   4   2

What's Your Name?

2   4   1   0   2

– –

Can you name the notes?

Let's Have Fun!

0   4   0   2   0   2   1

Silly Goose

Easy Peasy Lemon Squeezy

Lazy Cat

The Little Lighthouse

Shepherd's Hey

English Folk Song

Hello Upper 2nd Position on G string!

Greetings!

What's Your Name?

Can you name the notes?

Let's Have Fun!

Sleepy Sloth

Stargazing

Hello Upper 2nd Position on C string!

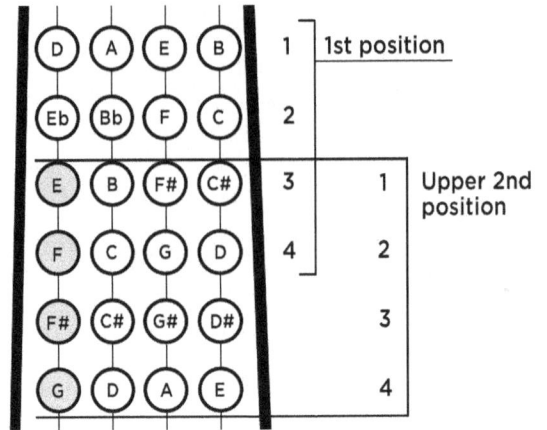

Upper 2nd Position

0   4   2   1   2   3   4

G   G   F   E   F   F#   G

Greetings!

What's Your Name?

Can you name the notes?

Let's Have Fun!

Silly Goose

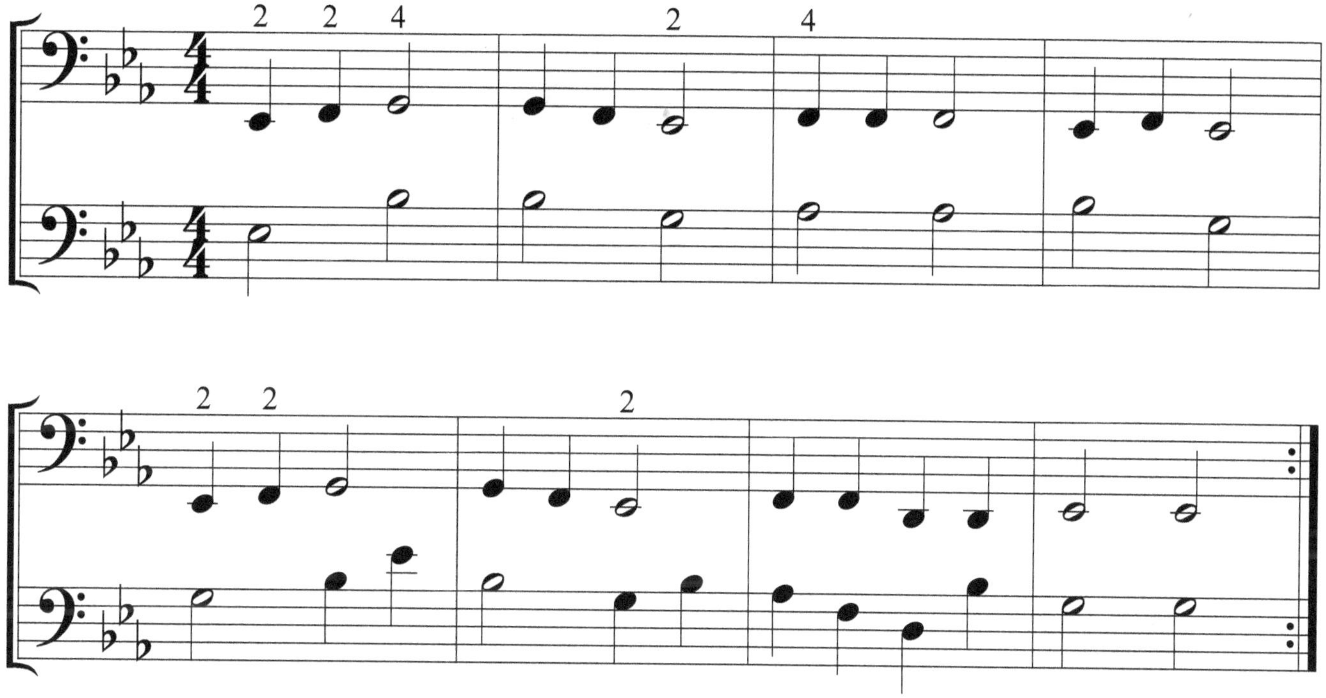

Lazy Cat

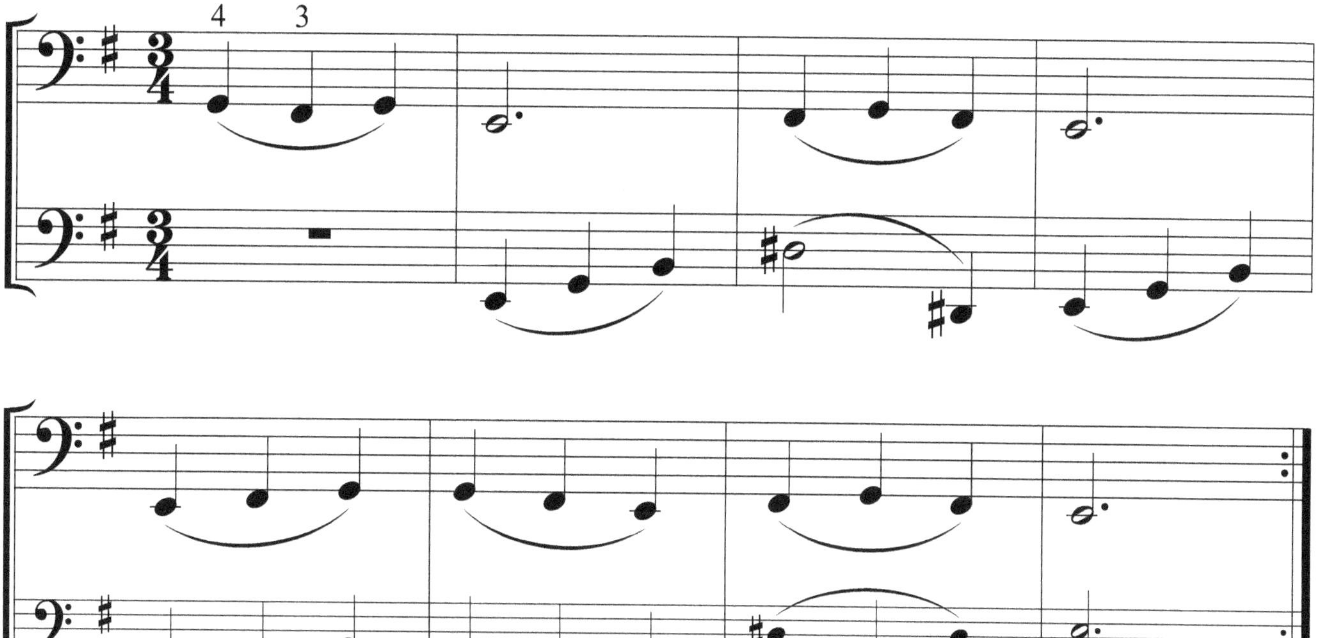

Skippy, the Baby Kangaroo

Owl and the Night Sky

Largo
from New World Symphony

Antonín Dvořák
(1841-1904)

Ode to Joy
from Symphony No. 9

Ludwig van Beethoven
(1770-1827)

Hello Extended 2nd Position on A string!

Extended 2nd Position

D   D   D   C   D   D#   E

Hot Cross Buns

Traditional

Mary Had a Little Lamb

Traditional

Can you name the notes?

Mini Adventure

Silly Goose

C sharp vs. C natural

Hello Extended 2nd Position on D string!

G G G   F G G# A

Hot Cross Buns

Traditional

Mary Had a Little Lamb

Traditional

Can you name the notes?

Mini Adventure

Cousin Jacques

F sharp vs. F natural

22

Hello Extended 2nd Position on G string!

C C C   B♭ C C# D

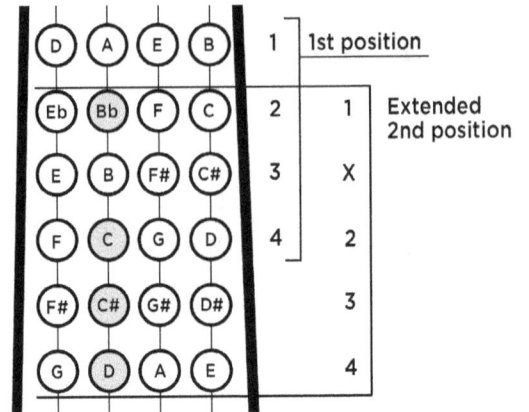

Hot Cross Buns

Traditional

Mary Had a Little Lamb

Traditional

Can you name the notes?

Mini Adventure

23

Very Sleepy Sloth

B natural vs. B flat

Hello Extended 2nd Position on C string!

Extended 2nd Position

0　4　2　×　1　×　2　3　4

G　G　F　　　Eb　F　F#　G

D	A	E	B	1	1st position
Eb	Bb	F	C	2	Extended 2nd position
E	B	F#	C#	3	X
F	C	G	D	4	2
F#	C#	G#	D#		3
G	D	A	E		4

Hot Cross Buns

Traditional

4　2　×　1

Mary Had a Little Lamb

Traditional

4　2　×　1

Can you name the notes?

4　2　×　1

Mini Adventure

4　　　4　　2　　　　4

Frère Jacques

French Folk Song

The Wheels on the Bus

Traditional

Hello Lower 2nd Position on A string!

Lower 2nd Position

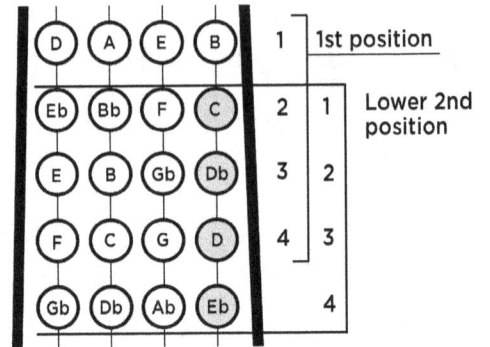

Rainy Monday

The Lost Duckling

Grandpa Jacques

Can you name the notes?

Little Goose

The Lonely Kitten

Hello Lower 2nd Postion on D string!

Lower 2nd Position

0 4 3 1 ♭2 3 ♭4

G G G F G♭ G A♭

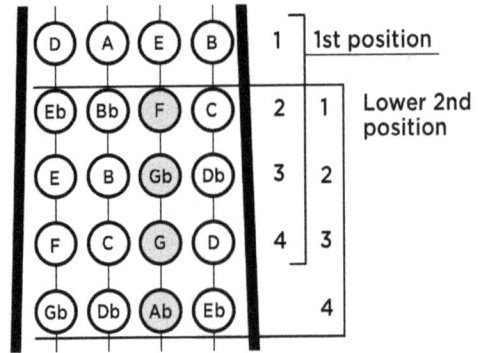

Rainy Monday

0 4 0 3 ♭4   0 4 0 3 ♭

The Lost Duckling

1 ♭4   1   1 ♭   1

Mary Lost a Little Lamb

♭4 3 1 ♭ ♭

Can you name the notes?

Minor Third Blue

The Loney Puppy

Hello Lower 2nd Position on G string!

Lower 2nd Position

C   C   C   Bb   B   C   Db

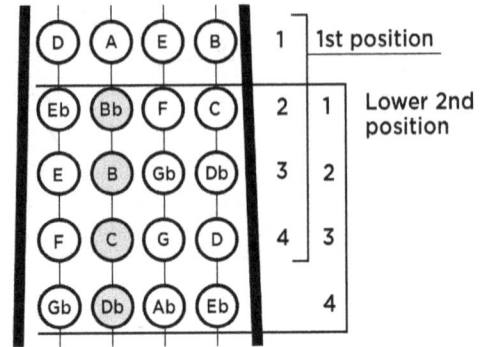

Rainy Monday

The Lost Duckling

Grandpa Jacques

Can you name the notes?

31

Little Goose

Elephant in the Circus

Hello Lower 2nd Position on C string!

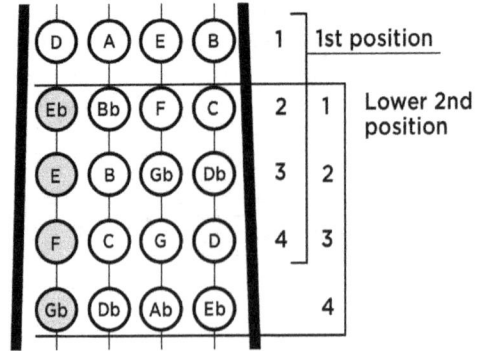

Lower 2nd Position

F   F   Eb E   F   Gb

Rainy Monday

The Lost Duckling

Mary Lost a Little Lamb

Can you name the notes?

Lazy Cat

Dancing Brown Bear

34

2nd Position Review Party!

This Old Man

Traditional

Jingle Bells

James Lord Pierpont
(1822-1893)

Wild Rabbit

Korean Folk Song

Morning
from Peer Gynt

Edvard Grieg
(1843-1907)

The Muffin Man

Traditional

Yankee Doodle

Traditional American

Little Horseman

Czech Folk Song

Circle Dance

Korean Folk Song

When the Saints Go Marching In

Traditional American

Emperor Waltz

Johann Strauss II
(1825-1899)

La Cucaracha

Spanish Folk Song

About the Author

As a Latin Grammy nominee, **Jisoo Ok** enjoys a multi-faceted and vibrant musical career as a cellist, festival director, arranger, orchestrator, recording artist and educator of classical and tango music.

Jisoo is deeply committed to exploring connections with musicians from other backgrounds and disciplines. This deep commitment can be seen in her collaborations with distinguished artists, such as latin jazz clarinetist Paquito D'Rivera, tango pianist Pablo Ziegler, bandoneonist Hector Del Curto, jazz violinist Regina Carter and bassist Ron Carter.

She has performed at prestigious venues and festivals, such as Carnegie Hall, Aspen Music Festival, La Jolla Music SummerFest, the Chautauqua Institute, Mondavi Center for the Performing Arts, Blue Note and National Concert Hall in Taiwan. As a soloist, she has performed with Rochester Philharmonic Orchestra and Lancaster Symphony Orchestra.

Her arrangements, orchestrations and transcriptions have been performed by top orchestras, such as Rochester Philharmonic Orchestra, St. Louis Symphony, Vermont Symphony Orchestra, Lancaster Symphony Orchestra, Billings Symphony Orchestra, Aspen Music Festival Chamber Orchestra and Stowe Tango Music Festival Orchestra.

Jisoo's dedication as a teacher can be seen in the success of her cello students, who have won numerous competitions and were accepted to Manhattan School of Music, New England Conservatory, Indiana University, The Juilliard School Pre-College, All-National Honors Orchestra and All-New York State Orchestra. She teaches privately and at the Virtuoso Suzuki Academy in Long Island, NY.

Jisoo was born in Seoul, Korea and raised in New Zealand. She received her Bachelor's and Master's degrees from The Juilliard School, studying with Bonnie Hampton and Fred Sherry. She studied chamber music with Itzhak Perlman and Robert Mann.

She is the co-founder and co- director of the Stowe Tango Music Festival, the premier tango music festival in the United States.

www.okcellist.com

www.ingramcontent.com/pod-product-compliance
Lightning Source LLC
Chambersburg PA
CBHW081304040426
42452CB00014B/2640